Ubuntu philosophy as a competitive strategy for women entrepreneurs in Uganda

Olga Margret M Namasembe

Publisher: Upway Books

Author: Ubuntu philosophy as a competitive strategy for women entrepreneurs in Uganda

ISBN: 978-1-917916-08-0

Cover designed on: www.canva.com

This book is a work of non-fiction. The information contained within is based on the author's research, experience, and knowledge at the time of publication. The publisher and author have made every effort to ensure accuracy and reliability, but they assume no responsibility for errors, omissions, or contrary interpretations of the subject matter. This publication is not intended as a substitute for professional advice or consultation. Readers are encouraged to seek appropriate professional guidance as needed.

Summary

This manuscript presents two articles on the African philosophy of Ubuntu and feminisms in African female entrepreneurship from the context of Uganda.

Multiple studies have been done on the African philosophy of Ubuntu, however few studies explore the philosophy from an entrepreneurial, gender and anthropological angle. The first study aims to contribute to bridging the gap by bringing fresh insights into how African women perceive income generation and how this relates to them as individuals and to the social environment in which they live. The results suggest a paradoxical interface between Ubuntu principles and African female entrepreneurship.

Furthermore, studies on the intersection and impact of feminist theory between education and women entrepreneurship in Sub-Saharan Africa are scarce. The second study seeks to close the gap by offering new perspectives into how gender in Africa impacts education and career (focusing on the agribusiness industry in Uganda). The results suggest a nuance to the rationale behind women's perception of education compared to that of men. Contrary to the belief that African women have a limited access to education opportunities, findings show that choice also plays a role in their future prospects.

Contents

Ubuntu philosophy as a competitive strategy for women entrepreneurs in Uganda

Abstract

Aim: The aim of the research is to explore the impact of the Ubuntu philosophy, an African philosophy that advocates for the spirit of collaboration over the spirit of competition on African women entrepreneurship. This research adds to the discourse on African cultures and societies and their economic practices within the context of Uganda.

Methods: Semi-structured interviews were used to gather information from 109 women entrepreneurs. These were agribusiness players who ran a variety of businesses, including street vendors, retail stores, and market stalls. Emerging ideas were examined and explored using qualitative content analysis.

Results: The findings show that success for women is not necessarily connected to competition but it is the expression of goodwill through the sharing of resources to create a success cycle. The challenges they face such as 'giving on credit' to reach the business performance they desire is also discussed.

Conclusions: While business fundamentally hinges on competitive advantage to achieve high business performance, the study demonstrates the opposite for Ugandan women entrepreneurs, who employ the cultural principles of Ubuntu to achieve the same goal. On the other hand, the philosophy presents challenges that may hamper successful women entrepreneurship.

Originality. Multiple studies have been done on the African philosophy of Ubuntu, however few studies explore the philosophy from an entrepreneurial, gender and anthropological angle. This research therefore aims to contribute to bridging the gap by bringing fresh insights into how African women perceive income generation and how this relates to them as individuals and to the social environment in which they live. The results suggest a paradoxical interface between Ubuntu principles and African women entrepreneurship.

Key Words: Ubuntu philosophy, women entrepreneurs, competition, success, Uganda.

Introduction

Capitalism has been the centre of economic growth since the European industrial revolution in the 19th century[1]. A quote from Eric Allison sums the importance of competition this way, "World trade means competition from anywhere; advancing technology encourages cross-industry competition. Consequently, strategic planning must consider who our future competitors will be, not only who is here today"[2]. Business research has always centred on the concept of competitive advantage as a pillar for success in business[3] . This concept constitutes the possession of resources that entrepreneurs in a similar industry do not possess and with these, be able to attract more customers to their businesses thus outcompeting others or even transforming the field of business or industry[4]. In both the global north and south, these resources may range from products, technology, business relationships and even customers[5].

The concept of competitive advantage was born during the industrial revolution of the 18th century with the widespread adoption of capitalism in

---

[1] Haradhan Mojajan, 'The First Industrial Revolution: Creation of a New Global Human Era'. *Journal of Social Sciences and Humanities* 5, 4 (2019), pp. 377-387.

[2] Stanislav Zábojník, Denisa Čiderová and Daniel Krajčík, *Competitiveness in international business challenges for the EU economies* (Wolters Kluwer, Čzech Republic, 2020)

[3] Abdulwase. Rasheed, Ahmed. Faroq, Nasr. Fuad, Alyousofi. Asma and Yan. Shuasheng, 'The role of business strategy to create a competitive advantage in the organization'. *Open access Journal of Science* 4, 4 (2020), pp. 135-138.

[4] Steingrímsson, J.G., Bilge, P., Heyer, S., Seliger, G, 'Business Strategies for Competition and Collaboration for Remanufacturing of Production Equipment'in Seliger, G., Khraisheh, M., Jawahir, I. (eds) *Advances in Sustainable Manufacturing* (Springer, Berlin, Heidelberg, 2011), pp. 91-97.

[5] Kamila Zelga, 'The importance of competition and enterprise competitiveness' (World Scientific News, 2017).

Europe in order to stimulate economic growth[6]. While research[7] shows that capitalism has its origins from the West, Africa's indigenous societies also participated in some form of capitalism prior to the influence of European capitalism as it is known today. For example, in many parts of Africa, cowry shells were used as money to trade goods and services between the 14th and 19th centuries[8]. Competition therefore is a founding principle for successful business performance because it increases a business's finances which are the main aim of business entrepreneurship[9]. While the global south engages the concept of competition in entrepreneurial activities as its global north counterpart [10] there are variations in the practice and/or implementation depending on business size and location. Businesses in the global north and multinational corporations in the global south practice competition through open contestations that may involve technology and high skilled labour[11] that satisfy the individual or personal gains of the owners. Criticisms against entrepreneurial capitalism however have had multinational companies lean towards Corporate Social Responsibility (CSR) to express good will and give back to the community[12] for instance through sponsorship of noble causes such as climate change initiatives for sustainable

---

[6] Lawrence Krader, 'The beginnings of capitalism in central Europe (Peter Lang, New York, 2020)

[7] Jeffrey D. Sachs, 'Twentieth-century political economy: A brief history of capitalism. Oxford review of economic policy 15, 4(1999), pp. 90-101.

[8] Alexis B. Tengan, Currency (Cowry Shells): 1400 to 1900: Africa (Sage,Dahomey, 2012)

[9] Sonia Felix and Chiara Maggi, 'What is the impact of increased business competition?' (International Monetary Fund, 2019)

[10] Organisation for Economic Co-operation and Development, 'Promoting SMEs for Development: The Enabling Environment and Trade and Investment Capacity Building' (Organisation for Economic Co-operation and Development, 2004)

[11] Bernhard Dachs 'The impact of new technologies on the labour market and the social economy' ((European Parliament Research Service, 2018)

[12] Eliza Sharma, 'A review of corporate social responsibility in developed and developing nations'. Corporate Social Responsibility and Environmental Management 26, 4 (2019), pp. 712-720.

economic development, clean water enterprises for rural populations and education scholarships for underprivileged children in society etc. However, CSR at the same time is used as a competitive strategy to stay ahead of competitors[13] or even monopolise an industry.

On the other hand, small and medium sized companies in the global south tend to steadily rely on the ideology of Ubuntu to compete as well as to give back to business stakeholders which practice is particularly observed among women entrepreneurs[14]. The ideology of Ubuntu or Ubuntu philosophy centres on goodwill, sharing, and togetherness of community in the social, economic, and political aspects of a society[15]. While CSR may only focus on looking good to the public on the outside, Ubuntu goes deeper to formulate individual identity that in turn affects a whole society or community. For example, given the high informality of African economies dominated by women in agriculture[16] the use of credit and trust are key mechanisms that women employ in business. "Credit giving or giving on credit" is a mechanism that they use to achieve financial support, where one's personal relationships with the owner can permit the business owner to sell them goods and allow them to pay later. While this is not unique to the African Ubuntu philosophy, the difference lies in the togetherness that encompasses the business relationships in Africa's informal business settings. This highlights the importance of collectiveness which draws a clear

---

[13] Chen. Youhua, Wen. Xiao-Wei and Luo. Ming-Zhong, 'Corporate Social Responsibility Spillover and Competition Effects on the Food Industry'. *Australian Economic Papers* 55, 1 (2016), pp. 1-13.

[14] Njeri K. Mary, *African Markets and the Utu-Ubuntu Business Model: A Perspective on Economic Informality in Nairobi* (African Minds, Cape Town, 2019)

[15] Hailey John, *Ubuntu: A Literature Review* (Tutu Foundation, London, 2008)

[16] Soledad Vieitez-Cerdeño, S., Roser Manzanera-Ruiz, and Olga Margret M Namasembe, 'Ugandan women's approaches to doing business and becoming entrepreneurs. *Third World Quarterly* 44, 7 (2023), pp. 1435–1454.

distinction to the credit structures[17] in the West which are mainly established on individualism[18]. Using semi-structured interviews from 109 women in business in Uganda, this paper seeks analyse the impact of the Ubuntu philosophy in African women's business entrepreneurship with the aim of understanding from an anthropological standpoint African women's business practices pertaining to competition as well as the influence of Ubuntu towards women's progress and its challenges to their entrepreneurship efforts .

---

[17] Hanan Morsy, 'Access to Finance: Why Aren't Women Leaning In?' (International Monetary Fund, 2020)

[18] Abdel-Fattah E. Darwish and Günter L. Huber, 'Individualism vs. Collectivism in Different Cultures: A cross-cultural study'. *Intercultural Education* 14, 1(2003), pp. 47-56.

Review of the literature

Ubuntu philosophy is a humanist African philosophy that is established on the values of respect, sharing, personhood and co-responsibility etc.[19]. While the influence of modern ideas that exalt individualism, personal happiness and fulfilment at the expense of community have influenced African cultures and economies as a result of a colonial past and neo-colonial present[20], the philosophy which advocates collectivism still holds ground in sub-Saharan African societies. In fact, this philosophy played an important role in the reconciliation process in South Africa during the 90s and is still a guide to peace and oneness in the nation[21]. The Ubuntu philosophy springs from the bantu-speaking communities of Africa that are predominant in the South, the Centre and the East of Africa[22]. According to Himonga, Taylor and Pope[23], the Ubuntu philosophy hinges on several key principles namely; communality, respect, dignity, value, acceptance, sharing, co-responsibility, humaneness, social justice, fairness, personhood, morality, group solidarity, compassion, joy, love, fulfilment, reconciliation etc. which principles should be the foundation of African identity. According to

---

[19] Chigangaidze K. Robert, Matanga A. Anesu and Katsuro R. Tafadzwa, 'Ubuntu Philosophy as a Humanistic–Existential Framework for the Fight against the COVID-19 Pandemic'. *Journal of Humanistic Psychology 62*, 3 (2022), pp.319–333.

[20] Fabricio Pereira da Silva, 'The Community and the Paths of Critical Thinking in the Global Periphery: The Cases of sumak kawsay/suma qamaña and Ubuntu' in Bourqia, Rahma and Sili, Marcelo (eds), *New Paths of Development. Sustainable Development Goals Series* (Springer, 2020), pp. 246-261.

[21] van der Walt, Johannes and Oosthuizen, Izak, 'Ubuntu in South Africa: Hopes and disappointments – a pedagogical perspective'. *Perspectives in Education* 39, 4 (2021), pp. 89-103.

[22] Christine W. Gichure, 'Human nature/identity: the Ubuntu worldview and beyond' (Strathmore University, 2010).

[23] Chuma Himonga, Mark Taylor and Anne Pope, 'Reflections on judicial views of Ubuntu'. *Participatory Education Research* 16, 5(2013), pp.372-616.

Mugumbate and Nyanguru[24], the Ubuntu philosophy symbolises the culture of togetherness, the sense of community and goodwill toward others. This belief in and practice of Ubuntu particularly in African entrepreneurship, expounds on the conventional way in which business operations are generally understood. According to Samkange and Samkange [25], 'a person is a person through other people' demonstrating that Ubuntu goes beyond individual/personal gain and competition. Prior to Western influence, Ubuntu in economics was practiced through the barter trade system[26]. For example, farmers that cultivated bananas traded some of their harvest with iron smelters in exchange for hoes, knives and pangas etc, demonstrating a need for each other and a complementarity of the trades[27]. In the context of entrepreneurship today, the practice of Ubuntu allows entrepreneurs particularly women to not only share customers with one another but share business premises as well. There is trust among women entrepreneurs that sharing resources with one another is critical to individual success in business because as it not only creates a success cycle, but it also provides a form of togetherness used as a support system to allow for financial success and equality among individual members but through group efforts[28]. Furthermore, there is affirmation that this practice allows for interdependence within an

---

[24] Jacob Mugumbate, and Andrew Nyanguru, ' Exploring African philosophy: The value of Ubuntu in social work. *African Journal of Social Work* 3, 1 (2013), pp. 82-100.

[25] Samkange J.T. Stanlake and Samkange T. Marie, *Hunhuism or ubuntuism: A Zimbabwe Indigenous Political Philosophy* (Graham Publishing, Salisbury,Harare, 1980).

[26] Toncheva Rossitsa, 'Barter System Signals Harmony in Causality', (4th International Scientific Conference, 2014)

[27] Alexandra L. Escobar, Ramón R. López, Miguel Ángel Solano-Sánchez and María de los Baños García-Moreno García, 'The Role of Complementary Monetary System as an Instrument to Innovate the Local Financial System'. *Journal of Open Innovation Technology Market and Complexity* 6, 4 (2020), pp. 141.

[28] Oelofsen Rianna, 'Women and Ubuntu: Does Ubuntu condone the subordination of women?'in Jonathan Chimakonam and Louise du Toit (eds), *African Philosophy and the Epistemic Marginalization of Women* (Routledge, United Kingdom, 2018), pp. 42-56.

entrepreneur's supply chain thus strengthening mutual respect, trust or understanding and loyalty between sellers, suppliers and customers resulting into success for those involved within the chain[29]

The Baganda of Uganda from which our research is based speak a Bantu language Luganda with a saying *Obuntu Bulamu* loosely translated to mean "live life with integrity, personal responsibility to others and sincerity which in practice is a determinant for entrepreneurial success among Ugandan women entrepreneurs. Familusi[30] further notes that culture in Uganda is preserved more by women than men due to women's role and responsibility of nurturing (as mothers) the younger generations and passing on cultural values that later define their identity and contribution to society. While similar ideologies such as CSR may ascribe a business enterprise as community oriented, Ubuntu goes to the heart and influences individual character that influences a society. Mangaliso, Mangaliso and Ndanga[31] observe that the concept of competition is understood differently from the Ubuntu women's perspective. The practice of Ubuntu by women entrepreneurs as a competitive strategy may not necessarily be competition against fellow business enterprises but rather a combined effort to overcome a common goal. 'Competition' in this sense is a strategy to achieve superiority or power over a common hindrance which could be in the shape of economic policies or societal expectations. On the other hand, they further argue that Ubuntu may present a set of challenges which may arise as a result of failing

[29] Mfuniselwa J. Bhengu, ' Ubuntu locus in the Christian church in Africa', *MJ Bhengu's intellectual space,* 3 June 2013, https://jbhengu.wordpress.com/2014/01/09/the-locus-of-ubuntu-within-the-christian-church-in-africa/ (29 August 2024)

[30] Familusi O. Olumuyiwa, 'African Culture and the Status of Women: The Yoruba Example' (University of Ibadan, 2019)

[31] Mangaliso P.Mzamo, Mangaliso A. Nomazengele, Ndanga Z.B. Leah and Howard Jean-Denis, 'Contextualizing Organizational Change Management in Africa: Incorporating the Core Values of Ubuntu'. *Journal of African Business* 23, 4 (2021), 1029-1048.

to reconcile modern ways of doing business with African Ubuntu principles for example in customer relationships. Due to neo-colonial influences there may be women entrepreneurs not practicing Ubuntu in business despite previous observations and as such, those that do may use it to make their businesses more attractive and favourable to customers by giving discounts, giving on credit and rely on the goodwill of the customers to pay and even tip thus using Ubuntu to compete against those adopting 'modern tactics'. Furthermore Oelofsen [32] asserts that the Ubuntu philosophy is egalitarian in nature, therefore it provides a platform for African women's feminism to flourish which gives them power over their incomes hence confirming Nigerian-British writer Amina Mama's assertion that African women were feminists long before western influence on the continent.

According to Ntshangase and Matabane[33] gender inequality in Africa is premised as colonial ideology that misrepresents the African reality. African societies such the Baganda have always emphasized the concept of complementarity between men and women. On the other hand, the international gender debate emphasizes "equality" which in traditional African feminisms seems ambiguous given the acknowledgement of gender roles in African societies[34]. Gender complementarity then is key in understanding the African

---

[32] Oelofsen Rianna, 'Women and Ubuntu: Does Ubuntu condone the subordination of women?'in Jonathan Chimakonam and Louise du Toit (eds), *African Philosophy and the Epistemic Marginalization of Women* (Routledge, United Kingdom, 2018), pp. 42-56.

[33] Ntshangase, X. Mohammed and Matabane, J. Tihakodisho, 'The History of Gender Inequality: Analysis of Gender Inequality as a Colonial Legacy in Africa'. *African Journal of Gender, Society and Development* 11, 3 (2022), pp. 185-203.

[34] Mikidady, M. Mhando, 'Gender Inequality: An Alien Practice to African Cultural Settlement'. *Universal Journal of History and Culture* 4, 1 (2022), pp. 1-15.

conceptualisation of gender as sharing of power and not demanding of power[35] for example; the African feminism of negotiation *nego-feminism* advocates for a compromise between the genders in order to achieve a given goal[36]. Furthermore, the African feminism of *motherism* advocates a male-female complementarity that ensures the wholeness of human existence in a balanced ecosystem based on mutual partnership[37]. The philosophy of Ubuntu then draws direct parallels with these feminisms. For example*, nego feminism* by Obioma Nnaemeka[38] advocates for fairness and understanding between the genders; *Motherism* by Obianuju Acholonu[39] advocates for love for nature/earth, motherhood and nurturing by both genders and *snail sense feminism* by Akadi Adimora-Ezeigbo[40] advocates for dignity and fulfilment. Additionally *stiwanism* by Omolara Ogundipe-Leslie[41] highlights the impact of colonial and neo-colonial institutions (e.g. Education institutions) which were crowned with male influence which women in Africa have accepted at the expense of Ubuntu[42]. In addition, through these

---

[35] Muraina, L. Ọpẹ́yẹmí, and Ajímátanraẹjẹ, J. Abdulkareem,), 'Gender relations in Indigenous Yorùbá culture: questioning current feminist actions and advocacies'. *Third World Quarterly* 44, 9 (2023), pp. 2031–2045.

[36] Chauraya. Efiritha, 'The African view on gender and its impact on implemented gender policies and programs in Africa'. *Journal of Sustainable Development in Africa* 14, 3 (2012), pp. 252-261.

[37] Gopinath Khutia, 'A study of motherism in Chimamanda Adichie's half of a yellow sun'. *Research Journal of English Language and Literature* 8, 4 (2020), pp. 2321-3108.

[38] Nnaemeka Obioma, 'Nego-Feminism: Theorizing, Practicing, and Pruning Africa's Way'. *Development Cultures: New Environments, New Realities, New Strategies* 29, 2 (2004), pp. 357-385.

[39] Catherine Obianuju Acholonu, *Motherism: the Afrocentric alternative to feminism* (AFA publishing, Owerri Nigeria, 1995)

[40] Ngozi Ezenwa-Ohaeto, 'Reflections on Akachi Adimora-Ezeigbo's 'Snail-Sense Feminism': A humanist perspective. *PREORC Journal of Arts and Humanities* 4, 2 (2019), pp.1-11.

[41] Oluwakemi M.Olowonubi, Confidence O.Daniel, 'Women, Marriage and Choices in Olu'Dolapo's Omolewa. *Journal of Humanities and Social Sciences* 2,1 (2020), pp. 11-22.

[42] Kathrin Wolf and Michael Frese, 'Why husbands matter: Review of spousal influence on women entrepreneurship in sub-Saharan Africa'. *Africa Journal of Management 4* 1, (2018), pp. 1-32.

institutions African women have joined the band wagon of western and radical feminism movements which are or may be contrary to their cultural heritage[43].

---

[43] Amaefula C. Rowland, 'African Feminisms: Paradigms, Problems and Prospects'. *Feminismo/s* 37, (2021), pp. 289-305.

Study Methodology and Process

Semi structured interviews were conducted with different women entrepreneurs who practiced entrepreneurship and owned agribusiness enterprises that were located in Kampala and Wakiso in Uganda. Uganda was deemed a good research context because of its high rate of women in entrepreneurship[44]. Kampala is the capital city with a population of 2 million people. As such the rate of development is high particularly driven by agriculture given that agriculture employs 68% of the population and contributes 24% to country's GDP[45]. Wakiso is also a busy business center partly bordering Kampala.

These two settings are both located in Buganda in Uganda's central region and present a good context to analyze the Ubuntu philosophy in one of the Bantu speaking tribes in the country, them being the majority tribe in Uganda. The purpose of selecting two settings was to observe the full impact of the social context of women entrepreneurs[46] as well as taking into account the convenience of the location of enterprises for the researchers. In the beginning, the context was orientated and time was spent talking and engaging women entrepreneurs about their work and business environment. This means that women entrepreneurs were identified in market places, streets, shops and restaurants. They were directly approached for preliminary talks[47]. From this orientation work, respondents were purposively identified and approached and were engaged

[44] Ritah Mutuwa, 'Factors influencing the performance of women entrepreneurs in Kampala-Uganda (East and Southern African management institute, 2021)

[45] International Trade Administration, 'Uganda - Country Commercial Guide' (International Trade Administration, 2023)

[46] Joel Gehman, Vern.L Glaser, Kathleen M. Eisenhardt, Denny Gioia, Ann Langley and Kevin G. Corley, 'Finding Theory–method Fit: A Comparison of Three Qualitative Approaches to Theory Building'. *Journal of Management Inquiry* 27, 3 (2018), pp. 284–300.

[47] *Ibid*

in semi structured interviews[48]. Consideration was taken that their businesses were agribusinesses. The focus of our study on agribusinesses was due to women's dominance in this type of industry. Study respondents were self-selected and the total sample consisted (N=109) women entrepreneurs. Participants' individual characteristics varied across the following categories: type of business (market and street businesses, retail shops, restaurants, etc.), marital status (married 32, single 53, widowed 9, divorced 1, No response 14), family composition (2-4 members, 5-10 members) and business duration (1-20 years) and business location (Makerere, Naalya, Mulago, Ntinda etc)

Interviews of participants were conducted using both open ended questions with questions prepared prior to the interview[49]. The interview guide was developed with questions that sought to identify how Ubuntu principles where used by women in business, what circumstances encourage African feminisms as well as the challenges from practicing Ubuntu strategies. For example; women were asked their marital status, for what purpose they started business, what challenges they faced as well as possible solutions to those challenges. The interviews were carried out from 2019-2022 and were recorded by phone and later transcribed to help internalize the emerging concepts[50]. For example women mentioned being single and starting business to take of their families in the absence of the men which resulted in the exploration of the relationship between single motherhood, African feminism and the Ubuntu principle of dignity.

---

[48] Norman K. Denzin and Yvonna S. Lincoln, *The SAGE Handbook of Qualitative Research, (Sage, 2017)*

[49] Hyman R. Michael and Sierra Jeremy, 'Open- versus close-ended survey questions'. *Business Outlook* 14, 2 (2016), pp. 1-5.

[50] Julia Phillippi, and Jana Lauderdale, 'A Guide to Field Notes for Qualitative Research: Context and Conversation'. *Qualitative Health Research* 28, 3, (2018), pp. 381–388.

Data analysis

Using the conceptual framework of the Ubuntu philosophy principles as the analytical tool, the data was analyzed. This presented an interaction between the theories presented and the data from the fieldwork demonstrating a noticeable development between analytical stages[51] . The transcribed interviews and field notes were organized and coded using qualitative content analysis where concepts that had more repetitive[52] responses were selected to respond to the research questions. The questions asked included the following: a) what inspired you start business? b) What accomplishments are you proud of so far? c) Before starting this business, did you get any information or advice from anyone on how to start and sustain business? d) What are you doing different from your competitors? e) What challenges are facing currently? f) How are you overcoming these challenges and how would you advice other women to overcome them? The responses were then combined and connected in multiple levels (see Table 1 for an example of how a quote went through the analysis process). In the analysis process we constructed narratives through conversations[53] which supported the interpretation of the findings.

---

[51] Alvesson Mats and Sköldberg Kaj, *Reflexive Methodology: New Vistas for Qualitative Research* (Sage, Carlifonia, 2000)

[52] Hsieh Hsiu-Fang and Shannon E. Sarah, 'Three Approaches to Qualitative Content Analysis'. *Qualitative Health Research* 15, 9 (2005), pp. 1277–1288.

[53] Glaser G. Barney and Strauss L. Anselm, *The Discovery of Grounded Theory: Strategies for Qualitative Research* (Aldine, Chicago, 1967)

Table 1: Illustrating how a quote advanced through the analysis process

Quote to be analyzed	First round of coding	Second round	Ubuntu principles	Emerging narrative/Process
(…) no competition among us. We sell together as a group. Whoever gets the chance it's their day. We give customers choice, we have mangoes from Kenya and from here but mangoes from here are out of season so we are selling mainly from Kenya (…) We are strong together irrespective of how much each earns. (Respondent 10)	- No competitive spirit. - Group selling - Working together - Group opportunities - Customer choice - Money isn't hyped at the expense of group dynamics - Business luck	- Strong team spirit - Interdependence on each other to achieve business goals. - Individual benefits come from group work - Customer oriented.	-Communality -Group solidarity over competition for money -Sharing - Togetherness/Oneness -Group identity	Ubuntu principles vs competition in Women's daily business operations

The next section presents the three narratives or themes that emerged from the analysis. They are classified as: -. a) Ubuntu principles and competition in business operations in African women's entrepreneurship. b) Ubuntu principles and African feminisms, c) Gender complementarity among men and women, d) Challenges of Ubuntu in African Women's entrepreneurship.

Results and Analysis

This section presents the findings of the research following the research question how Ubuntu philosophy is used as a competitive strategy by business women in agriculture in Uganda. The findings are multi fold demonstrating the understanding of Ubuntu and business in an African setting. Furthermore, the analysis brings to light how this understanding fits into the bigger picture of the gender discourse pertaining to gender equality from an African perspective as well as the anthropological and business connotations there in.

Ubuntu principles and competition in business operations in African women's entrepreneurship

Results show that Ubuntu is a mechanism through which business operations may be achieved in women entrepreneurship without the generic understanding of competition. Women entrepreneurs said they believed that making money in business was connected to being compassionate and kind toward each other and that by creating an environment of sisterhood through looking out for each other and through reciprocity was how their businesses flourished.

> There is no competition between us as such since we all want to make money to sustain our homes and lives. We help each other actually by monopolising a price. If a customer comes to buy from me and they feel that my price is high, they'll go to my neighbour whom we'll have discussed with to charge the same price to the very last women on the street, so the customer will buy and at least one of us will have sold. (Respondent 44-street woman)

> In any business one has to have a generous heart, for example if I do not have a product a customer wants, I have to be generous to direct the customer where they can find it. If you do not have a generous heart like this, your business will not grow. There has to be a connection between neighbours even if they do the same thing. If I do not have a product, I shouldn't let the money go like that when I know my neighbour has it. In return I expect them to do the same for me. (Respondent 93-Mobile money agent)

> Without our women's savings group, I would be out of business. The authorities consider us street women in business illegal. They just

drop on you abruptly, confiscate all the stock and you lose your investment. When the Kampala City Authority (KCCA) locks you up, it's the group that bails you out (Respondent 10)

The employment of Ubuntu principles of compassion and group solidarity have helped women overcome times of economic hardships imposed on them by authorities in form of penalties for operating informally in the Ugandan context. Additionally, the concept of competition is perceived differently through group versus individual effort[54] and having good will between women encourages positive business performance minus competitive tendencies.

---

[54] Mangaliso P.Mzamo, Mangaliso A. Nomazengele, Ndanga Z.B. Leah and Howard Jean-Denis, 'Contextualizing Organizational Change Management in Africa: Incorporating the Core Values of Ubuntu'.

Ubuntu and African feminisms

Advocates for nego feminism present African feminism as the practice of negotiating and/or compromising with patriarchal structures that may stand in the way of women's economic advancement[55] in a particular pursuit, in this case, entrepreneurship. The practice of negotiation by women finds men compromising thus finding themselves on board and in support of women's economic efforts. Both feminisms were observed through women's marital statuses.

Married women

> (…) I have been able to build our own house with my husband and my husband and I are now landlords (respondent 1)

> My husband gave me money to start business years ago to start myself up in business. (Respondent 5)

> I wanted to contribute to something at home like electricity bills in addition to what my husband was contributing. Also, my husband is not able to give me all I ask him for so I wanted to have my own money. (Respondent 6)

> I am able to support my husband's income. When he does not have money, I help out and vice versa. (Respondent 70)

Married women's awareness of their economic situations as well as their desire to work despite having providing husbands, do negotiate with their husbands who

---

[55] Obioma, 'Nego-Feminism: Theorizing, Practicing, and Pruning Africa's Way'.

in turn compromise on sharing the bread winning role with their wives thus increasing women's entrepreneurship that allows for mutual dependence[56]. The results show that men are providing room to co-exist with their wives' income generating activities. This aspect directly forms a relationship between the Ubuntu principle of co responsibility with the foundational pillars of negotiation and compromise in nego feminism[57] . The 'I am because we are' in Ubuntu and nego feminism has found men realising that the economic strength of their homes depends on combined efforts thus providing support to their wives. On the other hand, there are circumstances that single women may find themselves in that require an adaptation from interdependence with men and the societal expectations that men are providers. In this sense, women have to transform themselves into bread winners without waiting for male provision. Such circumstances include; single motherhood/parenthood and/or widowhood. Proponents of snail sense feminism[58] advocate for women's slow but sure adaptation to circumventing taboos that hold them back in today's modern society. Women have to calculate opportune times in patriarchal structures to advocate for and achieve their needs. Women responded that;

> My husband neglected the family so I had to work and provide. (Respondent 14)
>
> My husband died and I had no one to take care of the family. (Respondent 37)

The Ubuntu principle of dignity influences women to reshape their position in patriarchal societies. This adjustment often comes through no fault of their own

---

[56] Oelofsen, 'Women and Ubuntu: Does Ubuntu condone the subordination of women?'

[57] Obioma, 'Nego-Feminism: Theorizing, Practicing, and Pruning Africa's Way'.

[58] Amaefula C. Rowland, 'African Feminisms: Paradigms, Problems and Prospects'.

but must adapt to the situation to survive[59]. While society expects the male gender to provide for their wives, children and mothers, the reality is the opposite. Therefore the circumstances of single parenthood and widowhood provide women with the opportunities to change the status quo so as to achieve dignity through economic independence. Thus the rise of working women in business entrepreneurship in Uganda. While snail sense feminism has achieved gains for women in this regard, men on the other hand feel no responsibility toward their children but rather are emboldened to create a cycle of promiscuous behaviour further encouraging single motherhood.

---

[59] Olumuyiwa, 'African Culture and the Status of Women: The Yoruba Example'.

Gender complementarity among men and women

Results also show that married women work amicably with their husbands to have two bread winners.

I started my business to support my husband's income because in this economy it is difficult one bread winner. (Respondent 20)

My husband gave me capital to start business. He and his family own a farm. So he brings the fruits for there and I sell them (Respondent 52)

This demonstrates African women's understanding of gender equality as sharing responsibility in form of complementarity. This finding coincide with the argument by Ọpẹ́yẹmí and Ajímátanraẹjẹ[60] that African feminism is different from western feminism given that African women were equal to men before western concepts and therefore their original practice of gender in economics complement each other in the economy of the home.

---

[60] Ọpẹ́yẹmí, and Ajímátanraẹjẹ, 'Gender relations in Indigenous Yorùbá culture: questioning current feminist actions and advocacies'.

Challenges of Ubuntu for women entrepreneurship

The Ubuntu principle of kindness through sharing/giving is often observed among women entrepreneurs in Ugandan businesses with a saying *assubira akira aloota* translated 'one who hopes is better than one who simply dreams or wishes'. This principle is often observed through the act of 'giving on credit' to customers that may be in need of a particular product but may lack the funds to pay for it at the moment. Entrepreneurs will then sell on credit and believe in the hope that their credit customers will pay later. This may not happen due to economic hardships resulting into failure of business ventures[61]. When asked what their major challenges were in business, women said;

> Customers that do not pay. They come and ask for products on credit and do not pay (Respondent 37)
>
> Lack of customer care, giving on credit and lack of patience (Respondent 84)

The practice of giving on credit acts a stumbling block to the true purpose of business which is profit-making[62]. While it encourages good will in business relationships and customer loyalty, it hinders healthy competition between businesses because it is based on kindness and understanding making businesses yield less. However women suggested methods on how this could be overcome.

> (...) women need to give on credit when the business is well established not before or else it will fail (Respondent 1)

This solution suggests that women should operate their businesses under strict financial discipline or professionalism at least for the first few years to avoid

---

[61] Zelga, 'The importance of competition and enterprise competitiveness'.

[62] Felix and Maggi, 'What is the impact of increased business competition?'

failure. Not giving credit to customers may however seem a neo colonial practice which may result into competitive attitudes that may conflict with Ubuntu principles[63].

---

[63] Mzamo, Nomazengele, Ndanga and Jean-Denis, 'Contextualizing Organizational Change Management in Africa: Incorporating the Core Values of Ubuntu'.

Discussion, Contributions and Conclusion

This study set out to analyse the impact of the Ubuntu philosophy in African women's business entrepreneurship with the aim of understanding from an anthropological standpoint African women's business practices pertaining to competition as well as the influence of Ubuntu towards women's progress and its challenges to their entrepreneurship efforts. Four arguments are made; a) that the Ubuntu philosophy espouses African cultural values preserved by women in business operations. b) that Ubuntu is used by women to empower themselves by indirectly getting men and society on board, c) Gender complementarity among men and women and d) that Ubuntu presents challenges in business that inhibit business competition due to its principles of communality etc. Competition in business is founded in gaining money, customers or market share and superiority over others. While there maybe women in business who suggest this as a solution to women's Ubuntu challenges following modern tactics of doing business or as a strategy against counterparts, this study finds that the philosophy of Ubuntu can be used to achieve business gains such as customer loyalty given its foundation on oneness of business and people despite the challenges. This is through focusing on group solidarity and not through competition as it is known. In this sense, Ubuntu being a competitive strategy means that women gaining through business an edge over economic or patriarchal conditions and not necessarily striving for superiority over other women entrepreneurs. The study makes the following contributions and conclusions to the field of anthropology and gender/African women.

Firstly, the philosophy of Ubuntu greatly influences the business culture in women's entrepreneurial activities. Since women are regarded as teachers of society in the sense that they are the ones that maintain the spirit of oneness through family. This spirit is reflected in their business operations together with

30

other women thus influencing their identity as African women entrepreneurs which spirit may not be identified in the global north, hence this approach to doing business differently contributes a new perspective to culture and entrepreneurship by demonstrating the role Ubuntu plays in the formation of African women beliefs for business success. The practice of Ubuntu creates an identity of "africanness" that is unique to/in African women's business operations. Secondly, the principles of Ubuntu such as co-responsibility and dignity inspire the practice of African feminism, that is, Nego and Snail sense feminisms that take on an indirect approach to removing barriers to women's economic empowerment. The practice of these feminisms as seen in the study highlights a direct contrast between African feminism and western radical feminism (which advocates the total destruction of the patriarchy which may include destroying men's contributions toward their wives/women). While the African feminisms presented in the study are different in attitude toward the patriarchy, they take on a liberal feminist approach that seeks to empower African women through business but with minimal disruption to the social order. They seek to make women empowered and equal to men without conflict as influenced by the espousal of Ubuntu principles. This brings to light African/Ugandan women entrepreneurs' contribution to the pursuit of gender equality and the gains achieved through becoming entrepreneurs with or without male support using Ubuntu. Thirdly, the debate on gender equality has been diverse and still is an on-going battle within various feminist fields and movements. While the cause of the battle is the same and applies to women all over the globe, the contexts differ. African societies are still perceived as the most paternalistic in the world with strong patriarchal systems that seem unbreakable. This is for example seen through access to credit or financial resources[64] which favours men to operate

---

[64] Morsy, 'Access to Finance: Why Aren't Women Leaning In?'

large scale agribusiness operations and yet women are limited to small and medium sized enterprises even though in the same agricultural industry.

On the other hand, while there are women today that have access to finances and are operating large scale enterprises, their success could be attributed to male support in the framework of teamwork. The concept of gender complementarity is therefore key in African women entrepreneurship given the understanding of gender role differences that translates into teamwork. This teamwork runs intertwined with the values of Ubuntu "I am because we are" and translates into women's work in complementation of their husband's work and in provision of their children's basic needs. Work for economic gain therefore is fulfilled by both genders with no competition in between. For example, gender complementarity counters competition in business as it fosters Ubuntu principles of sharing and caring. Men or husbands use their resources to uplift their wives' economic positions by giving them the opportunities to work in the same business as themselves for the benefit of the family[65]. Similarly, women or wives do the same thing when their husbands are not earning enough and the joint family needs receive extra economic support. Thus the results demonstrate that the concept of gender equality is understood as gender complementarity or neutrality[66] [67] [68] [69] by Ugandan married women entrepreneurs demonstrated through Ubuntu

---

[65] Wolf and Frese, 'Why husbands matter: Review of spousal influence on women entrepreneurship in sub-Saharan Africa'.

[66] Ntshangase, and Matabane, 'The History of Gender Inequality: Analysis of Gender Inequality as a Colonial Legacy in Africa'.

[67] Mikidady, 'Gender Inequality: An Alien Practice to African Cultural Settlement'.

[68] Ọpẹ́yẹmí, and Ajímátanraẹjẹ, 'Gender relations in Indigenous Yorùbá culture: questioning current feminist actions and advocacies'.

[69] Chauraya, 'The African view on gender and its impact on implemented gender policies and programs in Africa'.

principles. Lastly, the study brings to light the challenges that women entrepreneurs face as advocates of Ubuntu in business with potential solutions. These challenges and solutions expose a gap between old and new methods of doing business. African Stiwanism attributes this to colonial and neo-colonial effects on Africa that introduced attitudes of 'professionalism'[70]. With the practice of Ubuntu, women businesses are perceived as pass time income generating activities and may fail to truly achieve financial performance as those that keep things strictly professional. This presents a conflict between ways of doing business which may require the practice of Ubuntu principles to be revised for women's businesses to grow. Striving to draw a balance between new and old could encourage creativity and innovation as opposed to group think or uniform ideas which would be beneficial to women's entrepreneurship.

While the philosophy of Ubuntu is slowly being discarded due to the western influence of individualism, key aspects of it are still evident particularly in the way women entrepreneurs do business. However, there is an effort to strike a balance between Ubuntu collectivism (sharing and togetherness) and staying afloat in business in manner that may or may not be competitive. Ubuntu principles play a vital role in ensuring this model of business in the African business context by encouraging sharing or resources for the benefit of those involved. This encourages sustainable supply and demand chains in business based on informal agreements that allow comradeship. On the other hand, while Ubuntu aims to share and bring people together under mutual respect, it may fail to guard against the pervasive influence of individual gain that destroys trust and gives room for 'negative' competition that often leads to business failure especially for small and medium sized enterprises. This hurts women more since they own majority of these enterprises compared to male counterparts.

---

[70] Olowonubi and Daniel, 'Women, Marriage and Choices in Olu'Dolapo's Omolewa.

Furthermore, the presence of male support goes a long way in ensuring gender neutrality in business operations. Married women tend to benefit more from this arrangement than unmarried women where men's resources are used in partnership[71] with their wives' resources to achieve a goal that impacts more people than just themselves.

The study concludes that the philosophy of Ubuntu does not encourage competition. However, it is a pillar for joint women efforts in business to achieve their business and personal goals. Additionally, while Ubuntu is a strong motivator for African feminisms, it also poses some challenges that could be resolved through deliberate attempts to strike a balance between known African values as well as new western business strategies for example a combination of professionalism and applicable Ubuntu principles. This article offers fresh insights into successful African entrepreneurship illustrated through the Ubuntu philosophy by women entrepreneurs. The Ubuntu philosophy symbolises the culture of togetherness[72] the sense of community and goodwill toward fellow business owners and other stakeholders. The belief in and practice of Ubuntu expounds on the conventional way in which business success is generally defined. Ubuntu goes beyond personal gain and competition, it allows women entrepreneurs to not only share customers with one another but share business premises as well. To some women entrepreneurs, sharing resources with one another is critical to individual success in business because it brings luck or fortune and to others this form of togetherness is used as a support system to allow for financial success to individual members but through group efforts.

---

[71] Wolf and Frese, 'Why husbands matter: Review of spousal influence on women entrepreneurship in sub-Saharan Africa'.

[72] Chigangaidze, Anesu and Tafadzwa, 'Ubuntu Philosophy as a Humanistic–Existential Framework for the Fight against the COVID-19 Pandemic'.

The culture of Ubuntu allows for successful business formation within agribusinesses with little to no requisite for exceptional educational achievement. While it is important for women entrepreneurs to have an entrepreneurship education experience to avoid business failure due to excessive 'selling on credit', Ubuntu allows for credit sales that build customer loyalty, a pillar for African women entrepreneurial success. 'Giving on credit' in the Ugandan context means that a seller or vendor can sell a product to the customer and the customer can pay at a later date. Furthermore, there is affirmation that this practice allows for interdependence within an entrepreneur's supply chain thus strengthening mutual respect, trust or understanding and loyalty between sellers, suppliers and customers resulting into success for those involved within the chain[73]. Finally, while there are customers and suppliers that take advantage of Ubuntu through cheating women entrepreneurs by failing to pay or by supplying them with rotten food supplies, the culture of Ubuntu and its benefits in maintaining a strong connection between businesses and stakeholders outweigh the negative influences in the long term due to already formed business relationships[74] (Samkange and Samkange, 1980).

---

[73] Njeri, '*African Markets and the Utu-Ubuntu Business Model: A Perspective on Economic Informality in Nairobi*'

[74] Samkange and Samkange, '*Hunhuism or ubuntuism: A Zimbabwe Indigenous Political Philosophy*'.

A Gender Analysis on the Educational Challenges That Women Entrepreneurs face in Agribusiness Entrepreneurship in Uganda

Abstract

Aim: In this study, a feminist analysis is made on the relationship between educational challenges and entrepreneurship among women and men entrepreneurs in the agribusiness industry in Uganda with the aim of understanding the impact on business performance.

Methods: 109 female entrepreneurs were interviewed using semi-structured methods. Street vendors, retail establishments, and market stalls were among the many companies operated by these agribusiness players. Using qualitative content analysis, emerging concepts were investigated and analyzed.

Results: Findings show that women are educationally challenged by a limited choice of business industry and a lack of business education compared to men. The probable causes for this are explained from a liberal, radical and multicultural feminist standpoint

Conclusions: It is concluded that while education positively influences women's business performance, there are nuances in the cause effect relationship between education and women entrepreneurship as analysed under feminist thought.

Originality. Studies on the intersection and impact of feminist theory between education and women entrepreneurship in Sub-Saharan Africa are scarce. Therefore, this study seeks to close the gap by offering new perspectives into how gender in Africa impacts education and career (focusing on the agribusiness industry in Uganda). The results suggest a nuance to the rationale behind women's perception of education compared to that of men. Contrary to the belief that African women have a limited access to education opportunities, findings show that choice also plays a role in their future prospects.

Key Words: feminist theories, women entrepreneurship, educational challenges, Uganda.

Introduction

Uganda has been applauded by the World Linguist Society as having the best English speakers and schools in the region[75] with school attendance of girls steadily increasing over the years[76]. Since women have been left behind previously due to colonial practices that exalted men in education[77], women empowerment initiatives have been exerted to avail equal access to education and economic opportunities to women[78]. Furthermore education has also opened the path for women to make their mark on the national economic sphere through entrepreneurship[79].which they have done through increased women entrepreneurship in the private sector[80].

However, despite these achievements, women still face a multitude of educational challenges in entrepreneurship that may be attributed to high incompletion rates[81] helping to explain their continued low business performance

---

[75] Michael Oduor, 'Uganda has best English speakers in Africa, *World Linguist Society*, 4 March 2017, https://www.africanews.com/2017/03/04/uganda-has-best-english-speakers-in-africa-world-linguistic-society/ (29 August 2024)

[76] Ministry of Education and Sports, 'The education and sports sector annual performance report 2011 – 2012' (Ministry of Education and Sports, 2012)

[77] Ashley E. Ricketts, '*Women's access to secondary education in colonial and postcolonial Tanzania and Rwanda* (Loyola University Chicago, unpublished Master's Thesis, 2013).

[78] Kate Ambler, Kelly Jones, and Michael. O'Sullivan, 'Facilitating women's access to an economic empowerment initiative: Evidence from Uganda' (World Development, 2021)

[79] Fernando Lourenço, Natalie Sappleton, Akosua Dardaine-Edwards, Gerard McElwee, David.W Taylor, Ranis Cheng and Anthony G. Taylor, 'Experience of entrepreneurial training for female farmers to stimulate entrepreneurship in Uganda'. *Gender in Management* 29, 7 (2014), pp. 382-401.

[80] Mary Komunte, 'Usage of Mobile Technology in Women Entrepreneurs: A case Study of Uganda'. *The African Journal of Information Systems* 7,3 (2015), pp. 52-74.

[81] Anne Mette Kjær and Nansozi K. Muwanga, 'Inclusion as political mobilisation: The political economy of quality education initiatives in Uganda' (Effective States and Inclusive Development Research Centre, Working paper No.65, 2016)

to that of their male counterparts[82]. Educational challenges in entrepreneurship are defined as those impediments that women face as a result of a limitation on their school experience for example a lack of proficient literacy skills caused by time and financial constraints as well as exposure to low quality education[83] . A study done by Kouakou et al[84] found that despite significant increment in women's participation in economic activities through entrepreneurship, men outperformed women in financial performance. The study found that businesses owned by men are 3.1 times larger and earn. 2.5 times more than female-owned businesses which may be attributed to the fact that men tend to take on more educational and business responsibilities than women do in terms of academic achievement and business operations[85].

Business performance is defined as the fulfilment of the financial and non-financial goals of an entrepreneur[86] measured in terms of capital, profits that support livelihood, and enterprise growth in terms of business size. Given this backdrop, this study seeks to investigate from a feminist standpoint what educational challenges women face in business with the aim of understanding the impact of education on the financial performance of women businesses. This paper is divided into six sections. Following this introduction is the context of

[82] Amy Copley, Birce Gokalp and Daniel Kirkwood. 'Unlocking the Potential of Women Entrepreneurs in Uganda: A brief of policy interventions' (World Bank, 2021).

[83] Hawah Nabbuye, 'Gender-sensitive pedagogy: The Bridge to girls' quality education in Uganda' (Echidna global scholars program policy brief, 2018).

[84] Koffi-Marc Kouakou, Vera Kintu Oling, Kareem Buyana and Mark Blackden, 'Uganda Country Gender Profile' (African Development Bank, 2016)

[85] Geoffrey Odaga, 'Gender in Uganda's tertiary educational distribution'. *Social Sciences & Humanities Open* 2, 1 (2020), pp. 100023.

[86]Awolusi O. Dele, 'The effects of successful outsourcing on perceived business performance in Nigeria banking industry: an empirical analysis'. *Research Journal of Business Management and Accounting* 1, 3 (2012), pp.046 -056.

the study, followed by the theoretical framework based on liberal, radical and multicultural feminist theories, the methodology and procedures used for the investigation, the results and discussion and lastly the conclusions, recommendations and areas for future research respectively.

Context of the Study

This study was carried out in Uganda, a country located in East Central Africa. The size of the United Kingdom, Uganda has a population of approximately 46 million. Historically, Uganda was a British protectorate from 1894-1962, attaining its independence on 9th October, 1962.

British education was introduced during the colonial era and has continued to be the standard for formal education in Uganda[87]. Uganda's Ministry of Education and Sports categorized the education system into four levels with sub-levels namely; Nursery school level, Primary school level, Secondary school, Tertiary level and University level. (See table 1).

---

[87] Rana Hassan and Wilson Macha, 'Education in Uganda'. 8 October 2020, https://wenr.wes.org/2020/10/education-in-uganda (29 August 2024).

Table 1: Structure of Uganda's Education System[88].

Education level	Age	Duration	Credential	Opportunities after Education
Nursery School	3-5	3 years		• Primary education
Primary School	6-12	7	Primary Leaving Exam certificate (PLE)	• Lower secondary (O level) • Technical school
Lower secondary (ordinary level)	13-16	4	Uganda Certificate of Education (UCE)	• Senior/ Upper Secondary (A' level) • Primary Teachers College • Technical / Vocational institutions • Agricultural institutions • Health institutions
Technical Institutions	16 and above	3	Certificate	• Technical Colleges • University
Upper secondary (advanced level)	17-18	2	Uganda Advanced Certificate of Education (UACE)	• University • Uganda University of Commerce • National College of Teachers • Uganda Technical University • Other training institutions
Primary Teachers University	16 and above	2	Certificate	National Teachers University
National University of Commerce	19 years	2-3 2	Diploma Diploma Diploma	- University - University - University
National University of Teachers		2	Diploma/Degree	
Ugandan Technical University		3-5		Post-graduate studies

Table 2. Enrollment rate and completion of primary and secondary education by gender[89].

	2008	2014	2016
Boys Secondary Enrollment Rate	54%	53%	No data
Girls secondary enrollment rate	46%	47%	No data
Boys Primary Completion Rate	50%	72%	60 %
Girls Primary Completion Rate	44%	72%	63 %

---

[88] Godfrey Ejuu, 'Early childhood development policy advances in Uganda'. *Contemporary Issues in Early Childhood*, 13, 3 (2012), pp. 248–255.

[89] Uganda Bureau of Statistics, 'The National Population and Housing Census 2014' (Uganda Bureau of Statistics, Education in the Thematic Report Series, 2017)

Given that Uganda is a mixed economy with private economic freedom and centralized economic planning and government regulation, the education system is further categorized into private and public education institutions. Private institutions provide education services that are independently funded for by the parents of the students while the education services of public institutions are paid for by the Government[90]. Private education institutions in Uganda constitute (57.1%) 17,859 schools at all educational levels while Public education institutions constitute (42.9%) 13,386 [91] [92].

While there has been an increment in educational achievement particularly for women, there is a considerable gap between the private and public education institutions which disproportionately impacts women. This is because according to research[93] women and girls face more financial constraints in pursuing a private education than men or boys taking the public school option (UBOS, 2017). However, due to implementation challenges such as teacher absence and competence appraisals in public schools, the quality of education imparted is not be in position to equip graduates with educational skills to compete[94] in the real world mainly affecting women. This study therefore seeks to explore the

---

[90] Saphina Nakulima, 'Privatisation in education and discrimination: its impact on the right to education in Uganda' (Initiative for Social and Economic Rights, 2016)

[91] Uganda Schools guide, 'Private Schools in Uganda' (Uganda Schools guide, 2022)

[92] Uganda Schools guide, 'Government Schools in Uganda' (Uganda Schools guide, 2022)

[93] Anna B. Ninsiima, Els Leye, Kristien Michielsen, Elizabeth Kemigisha, Violet.N Nyakato, and Gily Coene.), 'Girls Have More Challenges; They Need to Be Locked Up: A Qualitative Study of Gender Norms and the Sexuality of Young Adolescents in Uganda'. *International Journal of Environmental Research and Public Health* 15, 2 (2018), pp. 193.

[94] Sammy G. Poro, Andrew P. Yiga, Julius C. Enon, Marus Eton and Fabian Mwosi, 'Teacher competence and performance in primary schools in Nwoya District, Northern Uganda'. *International Journal of Advanced Research* 4, 1 (2019), 3-8.

educational challenges that women face particularly in the practical field of entrepreneurship.

Theoretical and conceptual framework

According to liberal feminists, the advocacy for equal access to education is as critical as the advocacy for economic opportunities for all[95]. This has been evidenced in Uganda's approach to publicizing part of the education system for all[96] to benefit women however this has led to the observation that despite equal access to education, women still lag behind with more men completing than women[97]. Radical critics of liberal feminism have criticized this approach to end women's discrimination in education as a reluctance to confront power and patriarchy which they blame for the continued gaps between women's and men's educational achievements[98]. On the other hand, according to radical feminists, the division of the education system into private and public leads to further limitations on women's educational experience[99].

Private institutions offer a better educational experience than the public institutions dividing men and women into the haves and have nots by financial means of which majority of men will acquire a better quality education than women[100]. Radical feminists attribute this to power dynamics which have been concentrated mainly on the masculine control of knowledge and culture and on sexual politics in the education system[101] irrespective of programs that seem to

[95] Amy Guttman, *Liberal Equality* (Cambridge University Press, New York, 1980).

[96] Hassan and Macha, 'Education in Uganda'.

[97] Geoffrey Odaga, 'Gender in Uganda's tertiary educational distribution'.

[98] Cheshire Calhoun, 'Taking seriously dual systems and sex'. *Hypatia* 13, 1 (2009), pp. 224-231.

[99] Marilyn French, *Beyond Power: On women, men, and morals* (Summit Books, New York, 1985)

[100] Anne Koedt, Ellen Levine, and Anita Rapone, *Radical Feminism* (: Quadrangle Books, New York, 1973)

[101] Sandra Acker, 'Feminist theory and the study of gender and education'. *International Review of Education 33*, 4 (1987), pp. 419-435.

desire to empower women. While liberal feminists advocate for a society where women's education is elevated as to that of men and access to economic opportunities are equally available to all in order to overcome women's educational challenges[102], radical feminists advocate for a society where putting women's and girls' concerns comes first before anything else[103]. Despite these solutions by the liberal and radical feminists, equity and equality seem to fail to bridge the educational gap since according to Krishna and Orhun[104] women are still found in so-called feminine education fields such as the arts and humanities with few women found in so-called masculine education fields such as architecture and engineering.

Although multicultural feminism arose from differences in ethnicity and race in the United States [105] its proposition of diversity between women and social groups is critical to understanding differences between women and men. Multicultural feminists argue that women's oppression this case in education is not necessarily because women face patriarchal obstacles as radical feminists believe but rather that it is a matter of differences between women themselves and men[106]. Spelman further argues that all women are not the same and their personal preferences and differences should be advocated for within feminist thought and not generalised as though women desire the same outcomes. For example women could choose not to pursue education and may choose

---

[102] Ernesto Laclau and Chantal Mauffe, *Hegemony and Socialist Strategy: Towards a Radical Democratic Politics* (Verso, London, 1989.

[103] Koedt, Levine, and Rapone, *Radical Feminism.*

[104] Aradhna Krishna and Yesim Orhun, '"Gender (Still) Matters in Business School". *Journal of Marketing Research,* 59, 1 (2021), pp. 191-210.

[105] Rosemarie Tong, *Feminist Thought: A more comprehensive Introduction* (Westview Press, University of North Carolina, 2009).

[106] Elizabeth V. Spelman, *Inessential Woman: Problems of Exclusion in Feminist Thought* (Beacon Press, Boston, 1988)

entrepreneurship instead even though the education and financial opportunities were available to them. Spelman asserts that women's decisions to do so should not be ignored in the quest for equality with men as liberal feminists propose. Additionally, Savage[107] Sorensen[108] and Peterson[109] argue that the biological/ psychological differences between men and women are clearly distinct and they influence gender choices and preferences. For example according to Croson and Gneezy[110], men tend to be attracted to things in this sense high educational achievements whereas women tend to be attracted to relationships in this sense starting a family and motherhood. The egalitarian societies in Scandinavia for example prove that the outcomes for both women and men in this sense education and entrepreneurship will always differ[111]. This is because irrespective of social constructs such as culture and global women empowerment efforts to make women equal to men, women will tend to choose a different path than men[112]. For example with education made available and accessible to all, women will tend to lean towards soft sciences and men toward hard sciences with a few exceptions. These preferential and biological dynamics influence the educational challenges that are observed between men and women in Uganda's education system as well.

---

[107] Maddy Savage, 'The 'paradox' of working in the World's most equal countries', *British Broadcasting Corporation*, 5 September 2019, https://www.bbc.com/worklife/article/20190831-the-paradox-of-working-in-the-worlds-most-equal-countries (29 August 2024)

[108] Astrid E. Sorensen, 'Gender segregation in the Nordic labour market: The Nordic gender equality paradox', *Nordics Info Arhus University,* 22 February 2019, https://nordics.info/show/artikel/gender-segregation-of-nordic-labour (29 August 2024)

[109] Jordan B. Peterson, 'The Gender Scandal: Part One (Scandinavia) and Part Two (Canada)', 7 December 2018, https://www.jordanbpeterson.com/political-correctness/the-gender-scandal-part-one-scandinavia-and-part-two-canada/ (29 August 2018)

[110] Rachel Croson and Uri Gneezy, 'Gender Differences in Preferences". *Journal of Economic Literature* 47, 2 (2009), pp. 448–474.
[111] Savage, 'The 'paradox' of working in the World's most equal countries'.

[112] . Peterson, 'The Gender Scandal: Part One (Scandinavia) and Part Two (Canada)'.

This theoretical framework highlights 3 key points. First, how liberal feminists advocate for equality or sameness in education institutions which is later evidenced in the work place in this case the entrepreneurship field, second how radical feminists explain the reason why women have educational challenges attributing it to strong patriarchal practices ingrained in society and third according to multiculturalism and how these challenges are not necessarily a result of the patriarchy but of gender preferential differences between men and women where women may not readily react by pursuing educational and economic opportunities that society expects them to pursue in an era of heightened women empowerment.

Methodology

This section explains various procedures that were used in gathering the data and analysis which are relevant to the research aims. The procedures are divided into segments such as the location of the study, research design, sampling and sample size, types of data, data collection method and data management.

4.1 Research Design, Strategy and Study area.

This study took on a descriptive research design which describes the characteristics of the study population. The data that was used was collected from women and men participants between 2019 and 2020 before the Covid 19 lockdowns in Uganda. This research design puts emphasis on what women's educational challenges are rather than why they face such challenges[113]. The data for this study was collected from women and men entrepreneurs in Agribusiness in Uganda. According to the two types of research approaches mentioned by Newman and Ridenour [114]namely quantitative and qualitative research approaches, the study took on the qualitative approach that used non-quantified data. The rationale for this was to derive meanings from participants' words pertaining to business management and operations to allow a feminist critique which may not have been possible with quantified data sets.

On the other hand however, a combination of both approaches was used in analyzing the data collected. The qualitative approach was used to extract interpretations from participants' verbatim and the quantitative approach was employed for simple mathematical computations such as tabulations and percentages. The study was carried out in Kampala and Wakiso districts. The

---

[113] Earl Babbie, *The Practice of Social Research*. Belmont, (Thomson/Wadsworth, Canada, 2013)

[114] Isadore Newman and Carolyn Ridenour, '*Qualitative-Quantitative Research Methodology: Exploring the interactive continuum*' (Southern Illinois University Press, Carbondale, 1998)

rationale behind this choice was that both these areas are metropolitan cities where participants necessary for the study were situated. The specific areas identified for the study were Nakasero, Ntinda, Wandegeya, Kalerwe, Kasenyi-Entebbe, Zana and Seguku-Katale.

Study population, sampling technique and Sample size

The population for this study was about 117 participants (109 women and 8 men). This included (65) markets, (20) streets, (4) restaurant owners, (21) retail shop owners, (1) greenhouse farmer, (1) seed vendor, (1) mobile money agent (2) vegetable farmer, Agriculture NGO (1). These were chosen based on their willingness to participate and proximity. Convenience sampling was used to select participants through initial conversations as preliminary tasks were conducted. Purposive sampling method was used to select the final participants that were included in the study.

Data Collection and Sample Limitations

In this study, semi-structured interviews were used as a way of data collection. These were used due to their flexibility and ability to enable the researcher stay on track. These involved predetermined questions as well as follow up questions. The interviews were done face to face and lasted 15 minutes to 1 hour due to the busy schedule of the participants. Primary data which was first-hand information collected directly from the field was used in this study. While the sample is quite representative of women, the pandemic lockdowns that ensued affected data collection from men entrepreneurs to a similar extent. The sample from which data was collected however is sufficient to achieve a correct representation of women's educational challenges as well as deduce subsequent conclusions.

Reliability, Validity of the Data and Data Analysis

Reliability was measured based on the internal consistency of the responses, that is, consistent responses which were repeated and observed across all participants[115]. Additionally, the interview questions were pre-tested during the planning stage to ensure validity by making sure that the results/responses answered the research question. Modifications were made before actual data collection for the purpose of measuring theoretical meaning and concepts, as well as deleting inconsistent, and redundant questions.

Content analysis was used to analyze the data. The categorization of themes and sub themes were derived[116]. The analysis of the data using this method helped us to narrow down to the results that addressed the research question. From the categorization, four main themes emerged in response to the educational challenges that women entrepreneurs faced in entrepreneurship namely a) women's versus men's education and entrepreneurship opportunities, b) the limitation on the choices of business industry, c) the limitation of financial and accounting education and c) women's individual choices and preferences. The next section presents these results and their interpretation in detail.

---

[115] Mark Saunders, Philip Lewis and Adrian Thornhill, *Research Methods for Business Students* (Pearson, Harlow UK, 2003)

[116] David S. Moore and George P. McCabe, '*Introduction to the Practice of Statistics* (Freeman & Company, New York, 2005)

Results and Discussion

Women's versus Men's education and entrepreneurship opportunities

Women and men entrepreneurs understood educational challenges to be limitations that impeded their ability to become employed in the formal sector or in jobs that required a lot of reading and writing. Men in agribusiness were found to have more educational experience than women entrepreneurs and the largest percentage of the study population had achieved only a primary level education (45%). The table below presents the results of level of education of both men and women.

Table 3: Percentages of level of education of women and men entrepreneurs.

Women entrepreneurs   Men entrepreneurs

No.	Variable	Frequency	Percentage	Frequency	Percentage
1.	No education	10	9.1%	-	0%
2.	Primary School Education	49	45%	-	0%
3.	Secondary School Education	33	30.2%	2	25%
4.	University Education	14	12.9%	6	75%
5.	No response	3	2.8%	-	-
	Total	109	100%	8	100%

Source: Field Work 2019/2020.

While the sample of men in the study is small, the data projects that both men and women are similarly educated as seen in participants with University education. According to Peterson[117] higher educational experience or qualifications propel them to take on larger business operations.

---

[117] Peterson, 'The Gender Scandal: Part One (Scandinavia) and Part Two (Canada)'.

The accomplishment that I am very proud of is the capital from the business which has helped expand the business three times over. The livelihood has significantly improved. (Respondent 115- Male University Retail shop owner)

Greenhouse farming is manageable and I can easily regulate it. It is also very profitable with high value crops. The biggest challenge is the cost that comes with modern farming but the benefits are good. I have expanded and I have built another greenhouse costing about Ushs.18 million (approx. $5,000). I have also gotten contacts in the business (Respondent 109- Female University Greenhouse farmer).

Entrepreneurship hinges on education to achieve successful business performance. Education experience irrespective of the gender of the entrepreneur greatly accounts for the success of one's business enterprise. This is attributed to the fact that a university education offers specific skills that may enhance one's entrepreneurial intentions[118] compared to those with none. These findings concur with liberal feminists who argue that women empowerment is met when women achieve access to the same educational and economic opportunities as those of men. In this case, women and men entrepreneurs with similar educational levels project a sense of uniformity between the genders within agribusiness entrepreneurship given the similar set of outcomes demonstrating that higher education positively impacts women's business performance.

On the other hand however, among women entrepreneurs with no university education experience, two major education challenges emerged from the results that impacted their entrepreneurship and business performance.

---

[118] Renato Passaro, Ivana Quinto and Antonio Thomas, 'The impact of higher education on entrepreneurial intention and human capital'. *Journal of Intellectual Capital* 19, 1(2018), pp. 135-156.

Limitation on the choice of business industry

Agriculture in Uganda provides opportunities for people with or without educational experience to make a livelihood. Results show that (84.3%) of women participants did not attain a university degree and chose the agribusiness industry for a lack of superior educational achievement.

> I chose to start business in the market because it is the easiest and most viable option for women like us who have little to no education. Also, the capital I had at the time was just enough to start a market business. It was not enough to start an educated business. (Participant 2-Primary education level)

> When my husband died, I had children to take care of. With only a primary 5 education, I worked odd jobs to make ends meet. Also I trained my children to work hard. They used to make chapati, sumbusas etc. which I used to make and would bring the money to me. So we survived and now, the youngest has graduated from Kyambogo University. (Participant 94-Primary education level)

Due to a limitation on their education experience, women are constrained to only be qualified to start businesses in the ubiquitous agribusiness industry. The limitation of education as well as the pervasive belief that they are 'uneducated' and so have to restrict themselves to Agribusiness majorly curtails them from pursuing economic opportunities in other industries leaving these industries for the men and a few women who may be more educationally qualified. This finding coincides with the radical feminist argument that the cause of women's educational challenges is the masculine monopolization of culture and knowledge[119] demonstrating that the labels women attach to themselves such as

---

[119] Acker, 'Feminist theory and the study of gender and education'

'uneducated' are a result of a discriminatory education system that elevates men and restricts women to specific economic opportunities undermining their business performance.

Nevertheless, liberal feminist advocacy for women's participation in economic opportunities in this case entrepreneurship should not be ignored given the fact that, it has promoted women in Uganda to take charge of their incomes and become bread winners as men. Through this advocacy, Ugandan women have become an entrepreneurial force to reckon with nationally and internationally. Although women believe that their choice of business is unworthy or limited since they do have a university degree, it has given them leverage to become at par with men in entrepreneurship which is something new in history since men have dominated agriculture previously. This is to say that while women may be limited educationally, they have achieved equity with men in agribusiness entrepreneurship.

Limitation of accounting/financial education

The possession of business skills such as balancing books of accounts is critical for the successful performance of a business. These help avoid business pitfalls that may lead to losses and ultimate business failure. The results show that women entrepreneurs are educationally challenged due to a limitation on their business skills revealed through cheating suppliers, lack of business experience, giving on credit and lack of the know-how of money management.

> The greatest challenge that women face in business is not knowing how to use money. One can use business money to meet other needs without calculating how it will impact the success of the business. One needs to use their profits for those needs but you may find one using all the profits and even the capital for personal desires. (Participant 37- secondary level)

> The main challenge I am facing currently is giving on credit and the creditors do not pay (Participant 39- primary level)

> We got a setback last month because we had saved with a sacco and they had told us that we save with them for a year, from January to now December. They told us to save whatever we could afford. But by November, they had closed the office without a trace. Many lost their money some 8 million, others 9 million and us 2 or 3 million. And we do not know where they went. (Participant 42-primary level)

> My challenge currently is losses (…), it is better to go directly to the food truck and get for yourself than to buy from the suppliers here because if you buy from here that's a loss, because they can sell to you already ripe food which is a loss. (Participant 45- secondary level)

These challenges are attributed to the fact that women face various gender impediments that inhibit their educational experience such as financial constraints. The public education system to which many women are beneficiaries does not offer an impactful entrepreneurship education as may be offered in the private education system. Radical feminists ascribe this to the patriarchal system controlled by men that divides women into those with financial means for a private education and those with no financial means for a public education. Women therefore are cumbered with the search for hefty fees to achieve private education to attain meaningful and impactful education experience that equips them with skills to thrive which may prove difficult given women's other economic and financial responsibilities towards their families, relatives and children. This may negatively affect women's business performance in the long term due to not having enough finances to make both ends meet.

Women's individual choices and preferences

Results further revealed that women make individual choices for themselves regarding the trajectory of their lives even when availed with so called 'equal opportunities'. What liberal and radical feminists believe should be of utmost importance to women in the struggle to achieve ultimate gender equality is not necessarily perceived as critical to some women entrepreneurs.

> If given an opportunity to go back to school, would you take it? No. It would not be bad but I have passed that age of books. My brain wouldn't handle much... school requires a lot of mental strength which I do not have at this age. (Participant 1- Female entrepreneur)

While she believes that education is good, she personally would not be bothered with it even if given the opportunities to pursue it further. Men on the other hand reacted differently.

> Yes education is important for success, when you read or when you get an education, even if it is not in business, up to tertiary level for example there are certain socio-economic aspects that you start appreciating than if you did not get the education (Participant 111- Male entrepreneur)

This shows the differences between men and women in regard to how they perceive the world. Both appreciate the value of education however while the male entrepreneur welcomed the idea of more education given its impact on understanding his business environment, the female entrepreneur welcomes the idea but is not up for the challenge due to mental ability and age. This result agrees with multicultural feminists who advocate for the emphasis on the differences between women and men to understand why they react differently to similar circumstances. In this case, women tend to make individual decisions taking into account their biological and preferential factors while men tend to lean toward more personal achievement demonstrating why men tend to prioritize and perform better in business than women.

Additionally, the results show that women tend to prefer smaller business to operate than men.

> Some women deliberately maintain small businesses to avoid the pressure and stress of managing multiple ventures. Whereas others believe in having multiple businesses to depend on each other, others would not have it. Ms. Murungi (not real name) a market woman wouldn't want another business except her market business because she has to work even if she is sick, so if she had other businesses, it would be a mess. (Excerpt from field diary 1st June 2020)

This demonstrates that women even when the opportunity as that of men appears may prefer to do things their own way in a manner that makes them comfortable. This establishes the multicultural feminist view that women are not homogeneous[120]. What women want is not necessarily what every woman wants and what scholars may view as a business performance problem is not necessarily perceived as a business problem or limitation to the women entrepreneurs.

---

[120] Spelman, *Inessential Woman: Problems of Exclusion in Feminist Thought.*

Contributions and Future lines for research

This study sought to investigate the educational challenges that women face in Agribusiness entrepreneurship in Uganda while taking on a feminist approach to understand the impact of the educational challenges on women business performance. The argument is made that women's educational challenges can be explained from liberal, radical and multicultural feminist perspectives. This study contributes to the field of gender and entrepreneurship in three key ways.

First, the results demonstrate that educated women and men with a University degree have similar outcomes in entrepreneurship or business performance demonstrating a win for the liberal feminist movements that advocate gender equality this way. This further reveals that the drive for women empowerment through education and entrepreneurship may indeed be achieving gender equality goals in Uganda. This is important because it shows that women can achieve their financial goals and contribute economically to society when given same opportunities as those given to men.

Second, although 12.9% are women entrepreneurs with high educational achievement as that of men, 84.3% are women without this privilege. They are educationally challenged in terms of choice of business industry as well as the lack of a business financial education. Given the patriarchal system that privatises quality education thus making it expensive for women with no financial means to acquire it while at the same time labelling and instigating women to label themselves as school dropouts and uneducated as observed by radical feminists. This system limits women's entry in so called educated sectors thus impounding their creativity dictating that they limit themselves to agribusiness and nothing more. This is important because it brings to light why educational programs developed to help women become empowered fall short of their goals.

Third, while women may face educational challenges, the reasons may not entirely be patriarchal as radical feminists argue. The reasons may be established in the biological differences between the genders as proposed by multicultural feminists. These advocate that what is perceived in feminist thought as 'educational challenges' may come as a result of women's preferences or choices as individuals and not as deliberate obstacles caused by masculine control in education and entrepreneurship systems. The findings have demonstrated that women may freely not choose to pursue further education even if the opportunities were availed to them and for this, multicultural feminists believe that women should not be treated as 'less than' those who have made the individual choice to pursue further education. This is critical because when it comes to women issues, one size does not fit all, referring to women as a homogeneous entity poses the risks of continued marginalisation and oppression in this sense ignoring some women at the expense of others.

It is concluded that indeed education has a positive correlation with entrepreneurship and ultimate business performance for women. However while some women are privileged to acquire it due to liberal feminist advocacy for equal gender opportunities in Uganda and be in position to compete head to head with men within the same industry, the majority of the women as revealed in the study do not possess such educational achievements which radical feminists attribute to unchallenged patriarchal systems. Although this may be so, women themselves may not necessarily perceive the limitation of financial education as an impediment to their entrepreneurship as men might due to preferential differences between both genders as evidenced for example in the egalitarian Scandinavian countries. The women's educational challenges of limited choice of business industry and limited financial education in Uganda can therefore be explained from different feminist contexts to understand how women's entrepreneurship is ultimately impacted.

Recommendations and Conclusion

This study focused on gender in the agribusiness industry in Uganda, further research could look at women's challenges particularly in industries labelled masculine such as manufacturing and engineering using a larger sample of male entrepreneurs.

Ethics declaration: The study involves human participants. This research was accepted to be done by the University of Granada, Spain and Makerere University, Uganda. Consent was derived from the participants and they were informed that their participation was confidential and would only be used for academic purposes. As part of the confidential agreement, their names have not been mentioned in this manuscript.

Acknowledgements: Special thanks go to Mr. Nicholas Balondemu from Makerere University who provided support during field research. Your support was inestimable. Thank you.